Amy,

I think [barcode] n
as monumental as your
wedding, it deserves
acknowledgement. I'll start
off by saying congratulations.
I just wanted to tell you
how proud, happy and
surprised I am for you.
For as long as I've known
you, I've experienced what
I'll call unconditional love –
never in all my years have
I met someone who loves
as fiercely and loyally as
you. All I've ever seen
you do is give, and for
that I will always be
amazed and humbled. So

When you told me you were getting married, I was so happy that you're finally giving in to having someone love you as much as you love them. Never have I met a person more deserving of the happily ever after than you. I know that in no way was your relationship perfect, but you're at a place where you make each other happy, and that's all I could ever want for you. And I'm so proud that you have finally accepted it and allowed it to happen.

You are truly an inspiration to me, Amy. I can only hope that one day I will be able to mirror your kindness, generosity and sense of self. At this point in my life I feel surrounded by

IT IS SOLVED BY WALKING

unknowns and pressured by needing to have it all figured out. But when I'm around you, I'm home. And I know that better, for worse and for the unknown that it will be okay. I don't know yet if you've realized it, but you have been an unwavering influence on my life that has truly helped me become who I am, but better yet who I strive to be. To be honest, I still haven't gotten used to not seeing you every day. I know it can't, but I sometimes wish things

Also by Catherine Banks
Bone Cage

could go back to how they were. And in a perfect roundabout of irony, I know that "Nothing Lasts Forever". But I find peace in the fact that when we can find the time to see each other, it's like nothing has changed. It has, but it hasn't. I can't thank you enough for letting me back into the

world I left; coming back and doing a scene this year has been something that I've looked forward to for months. I'm nervous. I owe all of my love for acting and all of my developed talent to you, and I hope more than anything that I can live up to the expectations. I know this is just one scene for a few weeks, but I haven't felt like I've done anything of consequence for the last few months, until this.
And I am so grateful to you for giving me the opportunity and for all

IT IS SOLVED BY WALKING
Catherine Banks

Playwrights Canada Press
Toronto

It Is Solved by Walking © Copyright 2012 by Catherine Banks

Playwrights Canada Press
202-269 Richmond St. W.
Toronto, ON M5V 1X1
416.703.0013 • info@playwrightscanada.com • www.playwrightscanada.com

For professional or amateur production rights, please contact:
Catherine Knights at Catalyst TCM
100 Broadview #310, Toronto, ON M4M 3H3
(p) 416-645-0935

We acknowledge the financial support of the Canada Council for the Arts, the Ontario Arts Council, the Ontario Media Development Corporation, and the Government of Canada through the Canada Book Fund for our publishing activities.

 Canada Council for the Arts   Conseil des Arts du Canada

 ONTARIO ARTS COUNCIL   CONSEIL DES ARTS DE L'ONTARIO

 Canada

 Ontario   Ontario Media Development Corporation

Cover art, *Red-Wing Blackbird* by Karen Klee-Atlin
Cover and type design by Blake Sproule

LIBRARY AND ARCHIVES CANADA CATALOGUING IN PUBLICATION
Banks, Catherine, 1957-
    It is solved by walking / Catherine Banks.

A play.
Also issued in electronic format.
ISBN 978-1-77091-044-7

    I. Title.

PS8553.A5635I8 2012   C812'.54   C2011-908745-6

Second printing: November 2012
Printed and bound in Canada by Gauvin Press, Gatineau

the experience you've given me in the past. I think you are such an incredible actress. You're finesse, you're tone and, to steal from this play, the sensation that you create onstage

is beautiful. You are beautiful. Inside and out. I've found beauty in the oddity of this play. "I do not know which to prefer, The beauty of inflections Or the beauty of innuendoes, The blackbird whistling Or just after." But I digress. At the end of the day, this is me wishing you

all the happiness in the
world with Jason. Embrace
everything about this -
you deserve it. I'm so
excited for the next
chapter of your life.
Thank you for being who
you are, you've been a
far larger part of my
life than you'll ever
know. Congratulations,
Amy.

All my love,
        Staci

It Is Solved by Walking premiered on April 28, 2011, at the Pumphouse Theatre, Calgary, Alberta, in a production by Urban Curvz Theatre. The cast and creative team for the premiere were:

Margaret: Laura Parken
Wallace Stevens: Allan Morgan

Director: Kathryn Waters
Stage manager: Emma Brager
Set design: Cimmeron Meyer
Costume design: Tracey Glass
Sound design: Allison Lynch-Griffiths
Lighting design: Alexandra Prichard
Assistant director: Angela Valliant
Technical director: Sabrina Miko
Producer: Michelle Kneale

It Is Solved by Walking has been translated into Catalan by Elisabet Rafols of Tant per Tant for Connexio Canadence 2012, a reading series in Catalonia, Spain.

Notes

It Is Solved by Walking is a play in thirteen stanzas inspired by the poem "Thirteen Ways of Looking at a Blackbird" by Wallace Stevens. Written before 1925, this poem is in the public domain, as is "Sunday Morning" and his essay "The Noble Rider and the Sound of Words," which are also quoted in the text.

Margaret, on occasion, calls up a memory of John and will speak to him as if he is present.

All stanzas/individual lines from "Thirteen Ways of Looking at a Blackbird" and "Sunday Morning" are italicized.

Margaret thinks like a poem, so her lines often look like a poem on the page with extra spacing for breath and lines of different length as needed for emphasis/intensity.

The ellipses used in Margaret's speech do not denote a hesitation or a dropped word, but serve to create an emphasis, rather like a rest between two notes in music. A single ellipsis (...) between words denotes that Margaret is trying to get her thoughts correct. Two ellipses (......) between words denotes that she is struggling to say something particularly painful and honest. An ellipsis at the beginning or end of a line indicates a thoughtful transition between the two characters.

When a line ends and drops down to the next line, it denotes a sense of waiting or that Margaret is going deep within.

Wallace is, of course, a voice in Margaret's head, and where their thoughts are tumbling together a dash (—) appears at the end of a line. There are no capitals on lines that begin with a dash to indicate thoughts quickly following each other. (As when twins finish each other's thoughts.)

Characters

Margaret—Margaret is not a faded beauty but grows into beauty during the course of the play. She is a believable fifty-three—greying hair, thickening waist rather than rail thin. She is a walker not a runner.

Wallace—Wallace Stevens as he exists in Margaret's head, in his mid- to late-fifties. Occasionally Wallace speaks lines belonging to John from memories Margaret calls up.

Set

The stage is divided into three areas.

Space One
The walking area. Margaret walks along a beautiful coastal path. There is a far point where the rocks jut out to meet the sea. Close attention must be paid to the walking route, as it is integral and must be fluid.

Space Two
This space is a second-storey platform centre stage. This is the interior, the place where poems are created, which Wallace Stevens often occupies and Margaret strives to get to during the play. There is a beautiful rosewood desk and chair. The desk is lit with a table lamp circa 1940, but above the space is the sky with the moon, stars and sun. Sometimes Margaret's walking route will take her under the platform and around the staircase.

Space Three
Margaret's bedroom. There is a double bed in the centre of the third space. A tall three-panel screen provides a changing area for Margaret. There is a large, elegant armchair with a low table beside it. On the table is a bowl of twelve large oranges, by stanza nine the bowl has only one orange remaining.

First and foremost this play is about light.

And for what, except for you, do I feel love?
    —Wallace Stevens, "Notes Toward a Supreme Fiction: To Henry
    Church"

but the doubly dead
who first went away
and then died,
like my husband—
those dead are harder to reach.
  —Miriam Waddington, "The Dead"

Sex is a beautiful thing—with your husband.
  —advice received at twelve

For whatever we lose (like a you or a me)
it's always ourselves we find in the sea.
  —e.e. cummings, "maggie and milly and molly and may"

prologue

The stage is dark. MARGARET reads the poem without emotion, as she would have read it her very first time at the age of seventeen.

MARGARET   "Thirteen Ways of Looking at a Blackbird"
by Wallace Stevens

I

Among twenty snowy mountains,
The only moving thing
Was the eye of the blackbird.

II

I was of three minds,
Like a tree
In which there are three blackbirds.

III

The blackbird whirled in the autumn winds.
It was a small part of the pantomime.

IV

A man and a woman
Are one.
A man and a woman and a blackbird
Are one.

V

I do not know which to prefer,
The beauty of inflections
Or the beauty of innuendoes,
The blackbird whistling
Or just after.

VI

Icicles filled the long window
With barbaric glass.
The shadow of the blackbird
Crossed it, to and fro.
The mood
Traced in the shadow
An indecipherable cause.

VII

O thin men of Haddam,
Why do you imagine golden birds?
Do you not see how the blackbird
Walks around the feet
Of the women about you?

VIII

I know noble accents
And lucid, inescapable rhythms;
But I know, too,
That the blackbird is involved
In what I know.

IX

When the blackbird flew out of sight,
It marked the edge
Of one of many circles.

X

At the sight of blackbirds
Flying in a green light,
Even the bawds of euphony
Would cry out sharply.

XI

He rode over Connecticut
In a glass coach.
Once, a fear pierced him,
In that he mistook
The shadow of his equipage
For blackbirds.

XII

The river is moving.
The blackbird must be flying.

XIII

It was evening all afternoon.
It was snowing
And it was going to snow.
The blackbird sat
In the cedar-limbs.

stanza i
the only moving thing

The stage is dimly lit.

MARGARET is in bed completely hidden under the duvet. Into the darkness comes the sound of MARGARET gasping to catch her breath. Her grief leads to a wail in a pattern of a woman coming to a sexual climax——it is the sound of death and sex.

WALLACE sits at his desk in the dark, smoking a cigarette. As the wail begins to taper he snaps on the desk lamp. He puts out the cigarette in a heavy crystal ashtray. He unscrews his fountain pen and begins to write on the pad of legal paper before him.

The light on WALLACE fades as it comes up on MARGARET's bed—— but still it is early morning——the dawn is only now breaking.

MARGARET surfaces and searches around under the covers until she finds and pulls out a well-worn copy of The Palm at the End of the Mind. *She props herself up with pillows, opens the book at random but she can't concentrate. Finally she throws the book to the floor. Some of the pages scatter and MARGARET gets out of bed, stuffing the pages randomly into the book. As she reaches for a page under the bed her hand brushes a white shoebox.*

She opens the shoebox, pulling out a beautiful beaded sari shawl of red silk. Slowly MARGARET wraps the shawl around her shoulders but is overwhelmed with its effect on her and she releases it.

MARGARET begins to pace the room until she is pacing under and around the spiral staircase. She stops, looking up. The sun is rising above WALLACE. It is the moment before the sun reaches the horizon. The red and orange light filters down between the floorboards, lighting MARGARET. MARGARET makes a fist and pounds on the unseen door.

The sound is huge and echoes.

MARGARET   Is there anybody there?

WALLACE stirs. There is the sound of a bird flying up and away. The sound is loud and echoes with MARGARET knocking on the door a second time.

Is there anybody there?

She stands listening intently as she looks up.

I came.
You didn't answer.
I kept my word.

MARGARET walks away. The scraping of WALLACE pushing back his chair stops her. She stands waiting as he descends the staircase, his footsteps measured and heavy with disapproval.

MARGARET often does not look at him. He is her personal haunt.
As he speaks the light changes to normal sunlight.

WALLACE   *(painfully)* "The Listeners?"

MARGARET   I can't... think.

WALLACE   It has been quite some time, Margaret. I almost didn't come.
               Nice touch, the sound effects I mean.

MARGARET   Since the call... I haven't been able to think.

WALLACE   But still *(dismissive)* Walter de la Mare. *(sighs)*

MARGARET   I can't think... Except for...

               WALLACE absorbs her thought.

WALLACE   *The only moving thing*

MARGARET   Not now... No... I don't want to think of that now.

WALLACE   Good line that.

MARGARET   Blackbirds, blackbirds, blackbirds!

               Why did you choose me?

WALLACE   *(moan)* That again.

MARGARET   You can't help me.

WALLACE   Not me. Never Wallace Stevens, lawyer, vice president of
               the Hartford Accident and Indemnity Company.

MARGARET   The poet, the Pulitzer Prize winner for poetry, 1955!

WALLACE   Oh that man can't help you whatsoever.

MARGARET   Blackbirds then? Fucking blackbirds then?

WALLACE   What horrible thought are you hiding, Magpie?

MARGARET   Stop it. My husband—

WALLACE   —long-dead to you—

MARGARET   —has been killed in a—!

WALLACE   —yes. In a tragic traffic accident. So why sex, Magpie?

MARGARET   No.

               No!

WALLACE   Sex.

               MARGARET moves about, restless with the possibility of this idea.

MARGARET   The poem cannot be reduced to epigrams…

WALLACE   …nor ideas.

WALLACE &
MARGARET   Sensations.

WALLACE   The first time, Margaret.

MARGARET   What, that I read it?

WALLACE   You felt it.

MARGARET   Answer my question first.

WALLACE   Why you?

MARGARET   Yes.

WALLACE   You will get to the end.

MARGARET   Ha.

WALLACE   Yes. Of everything.

                    He goes up the stairs.

MARGARET   You chose poorly!

                    MARGARET goes out of the house, facing a cold wind. She pauses.

                    (whispers) Among twenty snowy mountains,
                    The only moving thing
                    Was the eye of the blackbird.

WALLACE   *(formally) Among twenty snowy mountains,*

MARGARET   *The only moving thing*

WALLACE   *Was the eye of the blackbird.*

MARGARET wants to walk but she can't begin.

What is it you are waiting for?

MARGARET   I love this moment.

WALLACE   Yes?

MARGARET   This is the purest moment. The moment before the pen
             drops to the page to begin.

WALLACE   But that is a lie. It has already begun. It begins with the
             first thought.

MARGARET walks.

MARGARET   I remember that feeling... not that we had invented it...
             clearly there was sex in the world before we came togeth-
             er a bit drunkenly the first time, first date.

             If I stood, feet planted firmly on the bed and looked back,
             sex rises like a mountain range back through all of time.
             A chain of sexual peaks—

WALLACE groans.

Bad pun noted, Mr. Stevens.

Food, shelter, sex that's our only history. So we didn't in-
vent sex. We had been dating a few weeks when he had to
go to India. Not for work but his sister's wedding. I was
working, I was beginning to work on my thesis.

WALLACE   "Thirteen Ways of Looking at a Blackbird."

MARGARET   Stanza one. I was glad of the time alone, the time to think, to work. The day he came home… when I returned from TA'ing he was already waiting naked in my bed. He had brought a gift in a white box, a beautiful sari shawl of red silk like the women there are draped in on their wedding day. When I was naked and on top of him, his neck tasting of curry and cinnamon, he wrapped me in the silk… I felt wrapped in a membrane of…… why can't I find beautiful words?

> *MARGARET stops.*

This is nothing like a poem. I've waited too long. The words have flown, no, they are too heavy to fly.

WALLACE   Sensation, Margaret.

> *MARGARET walks on.*

MARGARET   This was the sensation. That no two people had ever fit together as our bodies did at that moment. I lay on the bed as he moves in me, the whole of the world outside frozen. The only thing is the movement of him inside of me. We are the only ones in the world since the beginning of time to move so. Achingly beautifully our bodies fit together so perfectly that to take them apart is to hear the sound of unlocking.

> *MARGARET makes a soft popping sound with her lips——rhythmically echoing the love-making in her head. She stops.*

And then as we both climax... surely there is a better word for that moment... my heart moves. My language is leaving me.

My heart... moves... in my chest as it has never before.

She pauses at the door.

John, I lay beside you, beside you, my lips glazing your ear and I whisper,

Among twenty snowy mountains,
The only moving thing
Was the eye of the blackbird.

MARGARET hurries back to her bedroom. She buries her face in the sari shawl and weeps—no sound, only the movements of weeping.

WALLACE returns to his desk and his writing.

stanza ii
three minds

WALLACE is dressed in full birding gear.

He looks around and peers at MARGARET through binoculars as she gets ready for a walk.

He speaks as though reading from a birding guidebook.

WALLACE   Blackbirds are solitary birds. The male blackbird establishes a territory during his first year that he will hold throughout his life. The territory is essential for pair formation and nesting. Territory boundaries break down when the adults moult. During this period, territory drive is very low and birds will feed outside their territories at abundant food sources.

MARGARET moves out of the house for a walk.

Say, at work or the gym or the faculty club.

MARGARET stops, clearly taken aback. WALLACE continues reading.

The male blackbird will re-establish its territory again in late autumn and defend it against all other blackbirds.

MARGARET walks on.

The male doctoral candidate is also territorial.

MARGARET stops.

She walks on.

The male English literature doctoral candidate establishes his territory by taking down his competition. If it is a male competitor he eats him while whirling his inferior's entrails over his head. Of course, if it is a female competitor he fucks her.

MARGARET gasps.

Thus the competition is eliminated and his territory is established.

MARGARET is unable to speak.

The candidacy exams just successfully completed, his, and the research trip, tomorrow, hers.

MARGARET walks on more quickly.

I was of three minds,
Like a tree
In which there are three blackbirds.

    Throughout, WALLACE will use his binoculars and make notes
    exactly as though he is observing in the field.

MARGARET longs to escape her mind / memory.

Seven forty-two a.m. The male wakes at the ready. Immediately he wants the female to engage in sexual relations. The female goes to the bathroom and carefully applies spermicidal jelly to her diaphragm and tucks it inside. There must not be a baby Magpie.

The male waits patiently, chirping from the bed that to have his candidacy exams behind him is amazing. He can't imagine being her with that near-death experience still ahead.

Seven forty-two a.m. The female is still only one set of candidacy exams behind the male. They make I'm-done-my-exams-but-you-are-not whoopee.

Ten thirty-six a.m. The male doctoral candidate…

> MARGARET *does not want this conversation in her head. She gazes out over the water. Slowly she begins to walk.*

Ten thirty-six a.m. The John reads from the letter inviting the Margaret to Hartford, Connecticut, to interview a dear friend of Wallace Stevens. John declares the man gay and a bitter failed poet because he mentions taking Margaret to a tea room for "elevenses" when she arrives and that he may have some surprising information on one Mr. Wallace Stevens, Esquire. They make I'm-so-glad-I-am-not-a-gay-failed-poet-living-in-Hartford-Connecticut-and-eating-out-on-Wallace-Stevens-stories whoopee.

One fifty-one p.m.

One fifty-one p.m. Where is she?

MARGARET groans.

The groan is involuntarily, as one does when a difficult memory surfaces. WALLACE holds up the binoculars.

Ah there Margaret is, at her desk working. John stands behind Margaret's desk chair as she checks through all her notes she is to take on the research trip. He begins the I'm-so-bored-Magpie-when-you're-so-busy ritual. He hints. He sings a little of "Sexual Healing." She laughs. He says, Please? They do *(pause)* it.

MARGARET has reached the far point.

Five thirteen p.m.

MARGARET   No!

WALLACE   Five thirteen p.m. On the kitchen floor. Unbelievable but duly recorded. She is to leave in eleven hours. There is something she will need but she doesn't know what it is, of course, she is in the act of forgetting. At this moment the female's private parts must be rather *(delicately)* raw?

MARGARET   On fire.

WALLACE   Eleven oh-nine p.m. She leaves in five hours. What, again?

MARGARET walks past him and crawls into the bed.

The male makes the plaintive call so familiar in the bed-
room before parting.

WALLACE speaks these lines like a bird call.

Will you miss me? Will you miss me? Will you miss me?

He curls behind her. He is cocksure, isn't he? She lifts her
knee, genitals aflame. He slides in.

What is she thinking? What is she thinking? What, Magpie?

MARGARET   Now he will know that I love him.

WALLACE   John, Magpie, love, up a tree k-i-s-s-i-n-g.

WALLACE folds up the chair.

MARGARET   It was love.

WALLACE stops.

WALLACE   And the crucial notes for the interview? Hours later
on the dark road, the road black slick with rain, you
remembered.

MARGARET sits up.

MARGARET   It wasn't raining... you and your embellishing poetics.

WALLACE turns towards her, slowly shakes his head.

WALLACE   Too late to turn back, you remembered:

MARGARET   I didn't ask you to be my...

WALLACE   ...imaginary friend?

MARGARET   Enemy. Your fan club is called the Friends and Enemies
            of Wallace Stevens.

WALLACE   Yes, I never strove to be beloved by all or even one.

            In those five couplings the female doctoral candidate falls
            one full year behind the male doctoral candidate.

MARGARET   Why did you choose that moment of no possibility of turn-
            ing back to take up residence here?

                MARGARET taps her head.

            John, Margaret, and black-hearted Wallace Stevens up a tree.

WALLACE   Because as any birder knows, blackbirds and academics
            cannot mate.

MARGARET   Then you should have left me years ago.

                The light leaks away from WALLACE.

            ...What? Now? Are you leaving me now?

                The light grows around him.

WALLACE   I am here at your pleasure.

MARGARET   You are here at my pain.

stanza iii
pantomimes

WALLACE lies shrouded in a sheet on the bed.

WALLACE   *The blackbird whirled in the autumn winds.*
It was a small part of the pantomime.

Pause.

The blackbird whirled in the autumn winds.
It was a small part of the pantomime.

He sighs deeply.

MARGARET enters. She takes off the raincoat, shaking it out.
Under her raincoat is a black silk nightie. It is short and
revealing but not in a sexy way, rather in an exposed way.

Lovely walking attire.

MARGARET wraps herself in John's housecoat.

MARGARET   I couldn't sleep.

WALLACE retrieves an orange from the bed.

I wanted to be her.

WALLACE   Who?

MARGARET   *Complacencies of the peignoir, and late*
             Coffee and oranges in a sunny chair.

WALLACE   Ahhhhh. "Sunday Morning."

MARGARET   Dr. Killam read it to us in my third year American Poets
             seminar.

WALLACE   The "What a splendid romp with words, Margaret, A+"
             Dr. Killam?

MARGARET   I used to like you.

WALLACE   The poem is not about a woman who keeps a bowl of or-
             anges in her bedroom.

             MARGARET changes the topic.

MARGARET   I had a dream last night.

WALLACE   Well?

             Tell me what it was about. You know you're dying to.
             Sorry.
             Three guesses?

             One. It is your defence, everyone in the room is clothed?
             Nude? You are nude? Clothed?

             Two. You're on an airplane that won't leave the ground?
             The air?

MARGARET   Once I thought you'd come to anoint me.

WALLACE   You insist on these roles, brute/martyr, that's the bore,
            and we were never married.

MARGARET   I would have divorced you.

WALLACE   Oh I know, years ago.

MARGARET   But you're a Catholic… Ha.

WALLACE   There you go again trying to make this about me.

                    She withdraws to recover.

MARGARET   In my dream he said, "I want to come back."

WALLACE   Three. It was John from beyond…

            So he wanted to come back. So?

MARGARET   It's metaphysical.

WALLACE   Define, Magpie.

MARGARET   Metaphysical, an uncommon noun, a type of nose clip
            used by Himalayan sheep farmers to prevent the stench
            of rutting males from entering their left nasal passage.

WALLACE   Ahhh, the self-mocking bird.

MARGARET   Fuck you.

WALLACE   You can, you know.

MARGARET   Fuck a dead poet?

WALLACE   Dredge it all up. Go ahead, make the poem be about sex.

MARGARET   How can I when you never got any?

WALLACE   I have evidence of married sex my dear, a child.

                 MARGARET is stricken. WALLACE gets up from the bed. He is wear-
                 ing the upper half of a wedding dress.

                 The blackbird whirled in the autumn winds.
                 It was a small part of the pantomime.

                 The pantomime! The anti-hero puppet Punch and his wife
                 Judy evolved out of the "pantomime."

                 The large shadows of Punch and Judy loom above them.

MARGARET   Punch and Judy... the blueprint of conjugal rights.

WALLACE   Lovely j sound, "j" *(He smiles.)* as in "J"ohn.

                 MARGARET walks, gazing into the eye of the matrimonial bed.

MARGARET   A week after the wedding John said, "What about my conju-
                 gals?" "Fuck your conjugals," I laughed back. Conjugal rights,
                 ridiculous. We were in our twenties, it was the 1980s not the
                 1580s. It made us giggle, that word. Imagine that, daring to
                 giggle! It is unbearable really, how naive we were... how

we thought... I thought we'd escaped all that because for
our wedding reception we went to hear the raucous lesbian
rocker Carole Pope. That we were not entering that oldest
of stories, that we too were not bit players in our anti-wed-
ding wedding clothes, that the pantomime whirling around
us was not binding us in as securely as it had bound our par-
ents, whose marriages we laughed at too.

*She musses the bed as though two people have been making
love. She walks on.*

We had really beautiful sex five times in our eighteen years
together.

The morning after our wedding was one of those five.
We moved together oh...

MARGARET becomes lost in the memory.

WALLACE makes a small sound to call her back.

The details are indescribable even if I were the poet...

WALLACE   ...you were sure then, you would become?

MARGARET wretchedly nods.

In the dream, is that what he asks to come back to, that
pure moment of beginning?

MARGARET   Yes, when we didn't yet know that without eyes without
ears we had backed our way into—

WALLACE   ——the Punch and Judy show!

               Starring as Judy——

MARGARET   ——me.

               Judy shadow bows.

WALLACE   Punch——?

MARGARET   ——You know.

               WALLACE waits.

               John.

               The shadow Punch bows.

WALLACE   The crocodile?

               The crocodile appears.

               The crocodile, John's tenure.

               Punch holds up a stick.

               The STICK, time ticking out on Magpie's Ph.D.

               *The crocodile retrieves the baby, holding it in its vicious
               mouth.*

               And the baby is…

MARGARET   Wait.

             Words were the stick.

WALLACE   Words?

MARGARET   His words. He was through the hoop of fire, his words.
             His words had Doctor, always Doctor in front of them.
             Blackbirds were only a small part of the pantomime.

WALLACE   Yes.

MARGARET   You, Wallace Stevens, were, are still, the relentlessly grin-
             ning crocodile.

             Snap. Snap.

             And the baby is...... the babies.

> *There is the crying sound of two babies from the space above.*
> *MARGARET is hungry for that sound. She is pulled towards it.*
>
> *MARGARET circles beneath the spiral staircase.*

stanza iv
the promise

WALLACE slowly gets out of the wedding gear and the Punch and Judy shadows fade away.

WALLACE A man and a woman are one. A man and a woman are one.

A man and a woman
Are one.
A man and a woman and a blackbird
Are one.

MARGARET quickly grabs what she needs for a walk and heads out the door. She is walking away from a demon.

MARGARET The best orgasms of the marriage were during my *(it is hard to say this in plural)* pregnancies... My body shimmered with them. Every nerve ending leapt up, vibrating like a blind earthworm coming out of the earth to feel the sun for the first time.

The first time, the sound that broke out of me could not be contained within the bedroom... it travelled through the ceiling... shot through the roof peak and sang its note all the way into the dark bed of stars... That sound...

WALLACE ...was most un-Magpie like.

MARGARET Yes.

She tests a sound.

Not anything like that. Not guttural, not smutty, not weak.

From that sound on I'm not Magpie anymore.

She pauses, looking out at the ocean.

I was only weeks pregnant. We had gone to the cottage to consider the... consequences of her, no, not of her... of me being so stupid as to get pregnant at the wrong time. The most wonderful sex of our marriage happened that night between John and me and Ladybird. It is as pure as what? a promise? yes oh yes. But he can't, doesn't feel her presence so really it is between the two of us... Ladybird, me.

My skin is charged... humming with the essence of our beings entwining... She asks for the promise and I answer her with that sound I couldn't have held back, even if I had known it was coming.

The points he makes during the weekend, and every point his eyes look, I answer with nothing. Ladybird chirps, "I am here, I am here, I hear."

The morning of the last day we stand in the bedroom and he asks, "So, what will you do?" and I answer,

A man and a woman
Are one.
A man and a woman and a blackbird
Are one.

He says...

MARGARET cannot go on.

WALLACE   You'll never finish now.

MARGARET   He leaves the bedroom, the cottage. I watch from the dormer as he flings himself down the path and this time it is raining... a heavy, drenching grey rain. He's gone for hours.

We are planning to be back in the city early but the afternoon is almost gone. Something tips, some ballast that I have been sure of shifts and I am suddenly afraid.

A message drops into my head... if I have this child he will leave me. A second message rolls at the feet of the first: if I don't have this child, he will leave me. But I nudge that thought out of sight... for years.

His mother calls up the stairs, "John are you up there?" She needs him to check the crawl space before he leaves. She thinks in the night she heard some animal cry out. "We can't have an animal nesting in the place, Margaret."

MARGARET touches her face, which reddens with the memory of those words.

I say, *(calling)* "John's not here but I will tell him to check when he gets back."

My answer a fissure, a tiny tear... a wound. "I am here," Ladybird chirps, "I am here, I hear."

Do you want to know the most painful human experience?

WALLACE   The undoing of something entwined in blood and bone?

MARGARET   The most painful human experience is to feel oneself—

WALLACE   —name things, my dear—

MARGARET   —to feel Margaret moving through the world and to see every consequence of Margaret's actions.

(louder) "John's not here but I will tell him to check when he gets back."

WALLACE   It was hardly a betrayal of Judas's proportions.

MARGARET   When is a promise a promise?

WALLACE   When it stops an action?

MARGARET   I hold the ladder as John, half disappeared into the attic crawl space, shines the flashlight into the womb-dark hole. There is no pretense in his jawline as he assures his mother that he can't see the animal that our... my actions are bringing forth into the world instead of...

WALLACE   *(tenderly)* ...a baby.

MARGARET   From that moment on Ladybird cannot find her breath in my womb. Before we reach the city the blood stains.

......John?

WALLACE   You've lost something hardly begun. We'll wait now until
             you've finished your Ph.D., Margaret.

MARGARET   Sex. Yes. But not to get pregnant again... No. No.

             Well, yes again, but far too late.

             Long after all things body and soul are unbearable.

MARGARET   Sexual drought does not mean there is no sex, it means
              there is absolutely no memorable sex. How did it go on
              for so long? So long, slang for goodbye.

              (thinking aloud) What word? The word. That sound. That
              word.

              Cosmo Girl, while counting the calories in my grocery cart,
              has all the answers of how to turn it up, turn him on. Hot
              sex on the count of five.

WALLACE   There is something pathetic or terribly beautiful, you
              choose, about a long line of frazzled, panicked wives
              furtively reading *Cosmo*'s sex tips in the grocery line.

MARGARET   Hey, want to hear something funny? There is something
              pathetic or terribly beautiful, you choose, about a long
              line of frazzled, panicked poets furtively reading *Cosmo*'s
              sex tips in the grocery line.

              Trying to understand why he wants sex when all she
              wants is five minutes for something, she can't just now
              think what.

              (mockingly) "Name things, my dear."

Trying to understand why John needs sex at all when all Margaret wants to do is think up one worthy line. "It's his stress reliever." "Sex is a gift that you give each other." "If you can get through the first five minutes, your body will respond, and then your mind will follow."

My mind is trying to hang onto one sweet line.

MARGARET begins to walk.

WALLACE   What lines are you finding today on your walk?

Let's start with what you see.

Birds. Animals. Blades of dune grass.

MARGARET begins the countdown of surrendering to sex.

MARGARET   FIVE! An ancient rabbit with his winter face.

WALLACE   An ancient rabbit with his winter face. The word "ancient," was that your first thought because it doesn't have the energy of winter face?

MARGARET   *(whispering)* I need to think.

WALLACE   Never mind, there's another, there is another line coming!

MARGARET   The ancient tree. FOUR! The ancient tree, supine in death.

John, please... No, I don't say anything because I can't say... I am thinking of the word for a poem that I will write. I will.

WALLACE   You've used ancient. Imply age. Think.

MARGARET   The...... grey tree. THREE!

               Starting to respond sexually.

WALLACE   Grey, really? No leave it. Go back to it later. Spruce? Pine?

MARGARET   I don't know. TWO! The tall thin ones with sparse needles.

WALLACE   Jack pine?

MARGARET   Hackmatack.

WALLACE   The grey hackmatack, supine...

               *MARGARET rushes through the door and flings herself into the
               bed. Lights low over the bed.*

MARGARET   ONE!

WALLACE   That isn't sounding bad, "supine" might work.

               MARGARET is in sex.

MARGARET   Yes.

WALLACE   Let's consider this word "supine." Lying face up, having
             the front or the ven-tr-al part upwards.

               MARGARET rolls over onto her back.

MARGARET   Yeees.

WALLACE   Palms up? Christ like? It's a good word but is it sublime?

MARGARET   Nice, so nice.

WALLACE   The best word isn't a nice word, it has to contain within
               it exactly the right sound combinations. Supine, sublime
               in death. Could work?

MARGARET   Yes. Yes. YES...... John!

WALLACE   Oh. Dear. God.

MARGARET   *(in a Groucho Marx voice)* Was it sublime for you too?

WALLACE   Choo choo. There goes that train of thought. Are you sat-
               isfied, Margaret?

MARGARET   Do you feel...?

               MARGARET stands at the foot of the bed.

WALLACE   What?

MARGARET   Anything. John!?

WALLACE   I will not have this.

               MARGARET pulls out of the memory.

               Do you even know where you are?

MARGARET   I am in Wallace Stevens's nightmare of a graduate scholar
               gone terribly gone.

WALLACE   *I do not know which to prefer,*
             The beauty of inflections
             Or the beauty of innuendoes,
             The blackbird whistling
             Or just after.

             Define "inflections," define "innuendoes," define "beauty,"
             in the context of the poem, in the context of your thesis.
             Yes, twice deferred, never completed, never defended.
             What is the sensation here?

                 MARGARET remains quiet.

             Accept it, accept this. You are not the poet you were go-
             ing to be, nor the scholar, nor the wife nor a mother. This
             grand pain over his death is only because you wish to be
             the widowed wife, no pressure, no defence, certainly no
             completion.

MARGARET   The servant chooses the brutality of the master by her
             level of non-compliance.

WALLACE   State the sensation.

MARGARET   The beauty of lovemaking or just after.

WALLACE   Ahh, for the first time you've use that word.

MARGARET   Because now sometimes we must make up love.

             The terrible beauty is...... we do.

stanza vi
shadows

MARGARET wearily stands at the door but she cannot go in.
Not yet.

MARGARET   I have been walking for hours. My pelvis aches with thinking.

MARGARET turns and walks to the far point.

WALLACE   *Icicles filled the long window*
With barbaric glass.
The shadow of the blackbird
Crossed it, to and fro.
The mood
Traced in the shadow
An indecipherable cause.

MARGARET leans into the air above the ocean, so easy to drop.

MARGARET   He hasn't bargained on marrying a failure. I haven't been
able to look higher than the knot in his tie for months.

WALLACE   Years.

MARGARET acknowledges that.

(simply) You are pregnant.

MARGARET moves closer to the danger of dropping over the edge of the rocks. She pulls back.

MARGARET   This is what I think. The body is a child and the mind is the adult. Sometimes the body gets pregnant but decides that it doesn't want the baby. The mind wants the baby. The mind is already whispering to the baby. But the body decides NO! and signals its intention with a bit of blood. The mind is horrified... it pleads... but the body is a child and won't listen and that is a miscarriage.

MARGARET walks on.

This is what I think. Sometimes the mind thinks, "I can't be pregnant. Not now. I can't!" But the body is a child and it holds the embryo like a marble in its fist. The mind asks, cajoles, but the body won't agree. And the body uses weapons like tender breasts already and subterranean orgasms.

But the mind has to deal with her unfinished Ph.D. And his silence, always his silence.

The body says, "Make me," and the mind does and that is an abortion.

WALLACE   What you think is an essay, what do you feel?

MARGARET   My mind didn't know that my body would be so wounded.

But the wounding of my body is nothing compared to the wounding of my mind.

MARGARET enters the house.

We didn't go the last six and a half years not having sex. At some point he must have got the courage to reach across the divide and my body, my mind, so wounded, said......
yes or maybe said nothing.

And so began the winter of our marriage, of unrelenting icicles in the wasteland of our emotional lives.

Everything in shadow. I was a shadow.

MARGARET's shadow lies across the bed.

Finally I gather my wounded self in. I walk.

WALLACE   You walk away...

MARGARET   ...from blackbirds. Yes. I walk...... I walk.

WALLACE   You walk a route. Every day you walk out the front door of your house but hours later you return, walk up the front steps, re-enter that life.

MARGARET   True. I walk in place until the distance between us, when we lay beside each other at night, is the distance between the two poles. Slowly our bed becomes a place of perpetual dark. The edges of our bodies, when they touch, are hardfrozen to feelings, behind our eyes... glaciers... that no words will ever penetrate.

WALLACE   Margaret, grief is not an indecipherable cause.

MARGARET   What is indecipherable is that I had not one poem to my name yet I say, "No."

No to everything.

I say, poem poems, poem poems, poem poems, poem poems, poem poems, poem poems, poem poems.

stanza vii
golden birds

MARGARET   There once was a middle-aged man from Haddam
who said, "Golden birds are delightful,"
shouting "blackbirds no more!"
as he walked out the door,
this most banal man of Haddam.

WALLACE   I adjust you, Margaret; to a middle-age man in a deadening life an erection is not banal.

MARGARET   "Adjust"?

WALLACE   I meant to say assure but by some trick or magic in the mind I said "adjust," which is more playful. It makes the word "banal" chirp.

MARGARET   Tell me about golden birds and men.

WALLACE   Perhaps it is a shortcut. Back in history a man like John would have joined the crusades, or jumped a Spanish Galleon leaving port, or signed up for some war, any goddamn war.

MARGARET   An accurate portrayal of what a man would endure to leave my bed?

WALLACE   *(whispers)* Feel that, portrayal teasing out betrayal.
(answering) Risking death is at least living, my dear.

MARGARET   The poet Wallace Stevens said…

WALLACE   I said…

MARGARET   *(correcting)* He said he just liked the name of Haddam. It
            could have been anywhere.

            Everywhere.

            Oh thin men of Haddam,
            Why do you imagine golden birds?
            Do you not see how the blackbird
            Walks around the feet
            Of the women about you?

WALLACE   Once he laid a red silk shawl beaded in gold on your skin.

            MARGARET begins walking, struggling to get to the top of the
            spiral staircase, the place to write, but failing.

MARGARET   We are in the dark of our early forties.

            There is a physical weight to these four words.

            I am not writing.

            He is Dean of Graduate Studies…… yet he's in the dark.

WALLACE   Committee work. Don't think, Margaret, that you ses-
            sionals know the half of it.

MARGARET   I can't think, I only do and do and do.

One day a golden beam appears… a light there, yes, there dead ahead, signalling an end to his darkness. He doesn't act on it. He is a married, married man married. But he has been infected with *(so difficult)* joy. He looks for this light everywhere. He no longer sees anything else. I can't think what is to be done. I am so fucking banal baking muffins with apples and walnuts.

He talks about other people's affairs obsessively as one does to make oneself invisible. Invincible.

He tells me… a cautionary tale.

WALLACE Get this, a guy notices that the Christmas lights on his neighbour's house are blinking in sync with the Christmas lights that his wife has strung on their house. He becomes obsessed with those blinking lights because, in his head, they are absolute proof that his wife is having an affair with their neighbour. Yeah, really. So the husband is diagnosed as having obsessive morbid pathological jealousy.

   MARGARET enters the bedroom.

The weird thing about this case was that, as it turned out, the wife was having an affair with their neighbour.

MARGARET *(to John)* So John, as it turned out, the husband was misdiagnosed.

The husband had, of course, seen the normal signs of an affair. A walnut in the bed, when I know I changed the bedding before going to work. But now, at bedtime, when

I turn down the sheet I see that someone, sometime after I left the house for the day, has been eating a muffin in the matrimonial bed. My eye catches... something golden glints... but I won't see that, I can't.

The only thing I can think to do is turn off the light.

The light grows more intense.

There, it has disappeared, hasn't it?

Anyway, the normal signs that he has been brushing off with a sweep of his hand manifests in the Christmas lights and the only explanation is infidelity.

I walk into the house, the cinnamon of the apple muffins still lingering in the air but the air feels different. Like all the molecules have realigned in some way I can't absorb the meaning of, but vaguely there's a feeling that someone unknown to me has been walking through my house.

MARGARET looks fully at WALLACE.

It destroys me still, John.

MARGARET stands at the bed.

I stand in our dark bedroom and watch you pull her hips in the air, watch you lay all your aching longing along the spine of her body, every part of your being communicating her goldenness to you.

What destroys me are the sobs that reverberate in my ears,

not mine, yours.

Your sobs enter my chest as surely as those tiny points of
light entered the pupils of the man watching his Christmas
lights blink in sync with the lights of his wife's lover. They
go on and on those sobs. I think...... you are crying out
all the sadness that is trapped inside this bed.

Then light floods it all away.

> WALLACE *touches the light switch, returning the lights to normal.*

I stare across the bed at you. You are not looking at the
turned down sheet, the bed raw, exposed and I ask.

My hand is already dropping to sweep away the walnut,
"Were you home during the day today?"

WALLACE   What are you doing in the dark, Margaret?

> MARGARET *looks at* WALLACE.

MARGARET   I don't repeat the question because right now sweep, sweep
I am deciding to live in the dark.

We have please-just-let-this-lie sex, in which I try to com-
municate what...? That time, long ago, when I was your
golden bird.

You try to communicate whatever-it-was-that-I-saw-is-
all-in-my-head.

Months later I shout at you, "She is just a golden bird, oh thin man of Haddam."

WALLACE   Fuck Wallace Stevens.

the blackbird is involved

MARGARET is working on a poem.

WALLACE watches her from his desk.

WALLACE   *I know noble accents*
And lucid, inescapable rhythms;
But I know, too,
That the blackbird is involved
In what I know.

MARGARET   The yardstick.

WALLACE   You make it so.

MARGARET   I read once that the great poets stand on the shoulders of lesser poets. If there were no lesser poets, you geniuses would not be the great poets.

WALLACE   A defence for mediocrity, dear Margaret?

MARGARET loves this verse, she says it with reverence.

MARGARET   *I know noble accents*
And lucid, inescapable rhythms;
But I know, too,
That the blackbird is involved
In what I know.

MARGARET crumples the poem. Then carefully smoothes it out.

WALLACE   Begin.

MARGARET tries to give the poem the benefit of the doubt.

MARGARET   Sometimes it would happen
             hours into our sleep
             we both would wake
             a spontaneous waking that I loved.

             Her exposure is unbearable.

             WALLACE indicates he is waiting.

             On that night I now remember into our bedroom
             came the sound of skateboards racing by our window
             a gang of boy-men taking advantage of the empty street
             to *do* it, the long hill beside our city house.
             We lay, not touching, listening as they swerved and swept by
             the skateboards' wheels' pulses or breaths
             the riders' voices' grunts, low whistles, whoops
             making me think of caribou pressing past
             tiny houses in the north following too
             some ancient mystifying radar.
             These man-boys thrilling to the empty dark street
             comrades in freedom and instincts.
             Or so it must have seemed to you although you only said
             skateboarders.

             That night as I lay beside you thinking,
             We are both awake!
             I did not know something was claiming you

that as the skateboards swept past
an aching thing rose out of you out of our bed out of the
window
and spirited our life away with it
even as I curled into your back cupping my hand over yours.
Even if I had noticed that light or shadow leaving our bed
I have learned in these raw years
that I did not then nor do I now possess the words
to call you back.

MARGARET begins to rip the poem down the middle.

WALLACE   You know my praise gives you no satisfaction.

She finishes ripping it in two.

MARGARET   It is messy in the middle, overwritten everywhere but
most especially at the end and it doesn't…

WALLACE   …"the riders' voices' grunts, low whistles, whoops
making me think of caribou pressing past
tiny houses in the north following too
some ancient mystifying radar."
Those lines have it.

MARGARET   Light? *(quoting Wallace Stevens)* "The poet fulfills himself
only as he sees his imagination become the light in the
minds of others."

WALLACE   Is there something you need me to say?

MARGARET   For your first poem in sixteen years—

WALLACE   —but this is the poem you wrote the day the divorce pa-
               pers arrived.

MARGARET   I've reworked it.

WALLACE   Ahhhhh. For your only poem in sixteen years, it is grounded.

MARGARET   When you say "grounded" you mean to say it does not
               make the leap.

WALLACE   A poem cannot be a frog in a jar.

MARGARET   How does a poem not be a frog in a jar?

WALLACE   In order to leap into the light, a poem, like the frog, must
               have space to—

MARGARET   —move forward into—

WALLACE   —exactly. *(thinks death)*

               MARGARET absorbs his thought.

MARGARET   No. In this poem he's not…

WALLACE   What?

MARGARET   In this poem, John is kept alive.

WALLACE   Well, there it is. All this time you have been revising a
               dead frog.

MARGARET   Must you be so cruel?

WALLACE   Margaret, apply electricity to a dissected frog's heart, watch
             its sickly beats and crow that you have a live frog—

MARGARET   —but don't expect it to leap into any goddamn space?
             So every poem now proclaims, he is dead.

WALLACE   Every poem knows that he is. That knowing is the light.

             She leaves the house, strides to the far point and throws the
             crumpled poem into the sea.

stanza ix
many circles with planets

MARGARET pulls back the chair and table to create a space in the room. She is building a universe in concentric circles.

She retrieves her high-school poetry anthology and places it in the centre of the floor. She walks round the book in a tight circle.

WALLACE moves out of the shadows.

MARGARET gets WALLACE's The Palm at the End of the Mind *and places it a little distance from the anthology. She walks, using the book as the beginning and end as she makes her way about the high-school anthology circle.*

MARGARET gets the white box, places the sari at an equal distance from WALLACE's poems. Again she walks around the universe so far, using the sari as the beginning and end.

WALLACE   What now?

MARGARET picks up the anthology and leafs through it.

MARGARET   My high-school poetry anthology. All my first loves. Larkin, cummings, Eliot, Bishop, Atwood, *(teasingly)* Robert Frost, Wallace Stevens, Walter de la Mare.

WALLACE   Please, if only one got to choose one's bedfellows.

MARGARET   Teasdale, Sexton, Plath.

WALLACE   Oh yes, the famously dead get read.

                She opens the high-school anthology to WALLACE'*s poems.*

MARGARET   Do you want to know what seventeen-year-old Margaret
               wrote beside your poem?

               "What are the blackbirds in Stevens's poem?"

                MARGARET *holds the page up to him.*

WALLACE   Oh yes, those years, when you wrote the "o" in poem in
               the shape of a heart.

MARGARET   I did.

                MARGARET *returns the anthology to the centre of the universe.*

                MARGARET *hauls out a large, clear plastic bag with shredded
                paper. She scoops some out and makes a ball with it, then
                carefully as before traces a circle from the ball around the
                sari circle.*

                *She moves to make a new outer circle. She stops, spreading
                her arms out slowly. She slowly walks around all the objects.*

                *She gets a blank sheet of paper. She holds it up to him. She
                places it on the floor and completes the circle walk.*

MARGARET retrieves the orange bowl, with one orange remaining, and places it a little distance from the paper.

WALLACE starts to speak but she silences him.

I was never a scholar.

Using the bowl as the beginning and end she walks around the universe.

MARGARET goes to the bed and strips back the bedclothes. She looks for and finds a single Rapunzel-length golden hair. She carefully lays it out. The hair is long enough to go completely around the universe so far.

She returns to the bed, taking the sheets off. She stands at the outer edge of the universe and holds a corner of each sheet in her hands to illustrate opposite poles.

Why is the familiar… how does the familiar become repellent? When I was a kid I loved holding two negative poles of magnets together. Feeling how determined they were not to connect. I brought the two negatives together again and again, to feel that sensation, that power of repelling. My heart would lurch when I forced the points to meet… the centre of deadness.

She lays the corners down so they do not touch.

WALLACE   And this is…?

MARGARET   The Universe o' Margaret.

WALLACE   Oh good, a science project, also decades late.

> *MARGARET walks over to him and takes his hands, leading him to the anthology.*

MARGARET   *When the blackbird flew out of sight,*
It marked the edge
Of one of many circles.

> *MARGARET hugs the anthology to her breast.*

Poetry.

> *They move to* The Palm at the End of the Mind.

The poet Wallace Stevens and all his beautiful poems.

> *MARGARET moves to the sari.*

John and Margaret in love.

> *WALLACE resists this so that she steps first and then faces him to pull him across the sari circle.*

John's Ph.D.

> *They laugh and step over the ball of shredded paper.*

> *WALLACE will in some way intrude on the next circle. MARGA-RET stops him.*

Stains.

WALLACE   Blood—?

MARGARET   *(nods)* —and of aborted first thoughts.

> *They step over the unmarked grave of that.*

All the poems I didn't write.

> *They step over the blank page.*

A married woman safe who keeps oranges in a bowl in her bedroom.

> *They step over the bowl.*

One Golden Hair.

> *They step over the golden hair.*

The last time we had sex.

> *MARGARET takes his arm, propelling him to step over the sheets. She walks the labyrinth holding the book of poetry.*

The last time we had sex, I, of course, did not know that it was the last time. Eighteen years of bad sex, good sex, great sex, indifferent sex… all the sex. Who really knows when, this sex, is the last time. People who are leaving for war think it could maybe be the very last time. Who else? So I didn't say to him, "This is the last time we will have sex." I didn't try to remember every second of it. No, the act of sex is an act of faith. We come home from the marriage counsellor where John has insisted that he does love me and I have insisted that I do love him. We have sex. Is there something else we could have done? Maybe. Sex is what we do.

Angry, mechanical, hurtful sex. He sucks too hard on my right breast because he is concentrating on getting hard enough to get inside of my resisting vagina.

Finally I say, "That hurts," and John says, "Sorry." He slips away inside his head. He feels her welcoming him and like that he is fully gone behind his eyes. But that's fine, because I've left too.

I am in the house we had when we were first married. I'm remembering the afternoon I arrived home before he did. I slowly walk through the downstairs, then climb the stairs, stripping off my clothes as I go, blouse, skirt, bra and on the top of the stairs my red-and-white lace panties. Naked I lay under the sheet on the bed that is showered in late spring sunlight that electrifies my sexiness. I am that girl again. I have fallen asleep and when I awake… right now… he is in the room, naked too, and he strips off the sheet and climbs above me. I open to him and he enters me so gently and we look into each other, me watching him, as he watches me. We soften, flush and climax.

Where did those two lovers go?

I didn't know the last time was the last time. But I remember finding his body next to mine repellent, his breathing repellent, having him undress in front of me repellent. I remember I said, "You can't sleep in this bed anymore." And he left our bedroom and a week later our house.

WALLACE   What is that, Margaret?

MARGARET   A story that might be a poem.

WALLACE   I'll give you this. It isn't maudlin. But. Is this really what
            you want to write for your start?

MARGARET   I want to be in the middle already with selected, collected
            works.

WALLACE   Not to quote that damnable Frost but, the road not taken.

MARGARET   I took that road every morning when I rose from our bed,
            but by the time I had walked across the campus to the shared
            office for non-tenure-stream English professors—

            *MARGARET walks backwards like a child retracing her steps
            in snow.*

WALLACE   —two thousand four hundred and sixty-four steps.

            *WALLACE steps behind her so that she bumps against his force
            field. There is no retracing those steps. She drops to her knees.
            In the fading light she gathers up her life and shoves it un-
            der the bed.*

stanza x
the point of turning

MARGARET is walking the path.

MARGARET   In the beginning we walked together. We walked miles of beach, not another person in sight, no evidence that we were not the only two people on earth.

WALLACE   Adam and Na-ive. *(stressing the "ive" to sound like "Eve")*

MARGARET   We were Adam and Eve, Adam and Eve before their story was distorted by the telling of it. There is poetry in that.

MARGARET stares out into the deep past.

WALLACE   What are you reaching for, Margaret?

MARGARET   A golden day.

WALLACE   How far back?

MARGARET   Three years before the year that marked the end.

We are on the beach for the afternoon... There is a storm, somewhere far out in the Atlantic, but we don't have it. We have a brilliantly sunny day and magnificent green, high-rolling waves.

WALLACE   A good metaphor.

MARGARET   I am not writing.

              The weight of those four words on MARGARET.

              We are walking. On that July day, a storm far out in the
              Atlantic, we watch a grey seal, caught in a great high-roll-
              ing green wave, the roller transparent, backlit by the sun,
              the seal stopped in green amber, a fossil of some joy once.
              The sea roils, spray leaps along the crest of the wave, the
              very centre of the roller solid, holding the seal a stilled
              heart. We go off into the dunes, the sun-drenched sand
              warm beneath us, the sounds of us coming mingled with
              the sound of the pounding of the waves along the shore.
              A golden day.

WALLACE   Tsk tsk—

MARGARET   Golden memories carry no more truth than the blackest
              memories.

              At what point does a liquid become solid? How long does
              it hold there just at the point of turning?

              The next morning in the car on the way home he wants to
              have sex. Suddenly he wants sex all the time, morning, noon
              and night. His erections are like a teenager's, ripe to burst.

              "What is it?" I do ask. He is so angry. "Can't we just have
              sex, does it all have to relate to words?" I answer with my
              body. I keep the pace. Still he wants more.

WALLACE   What do you feel?

MARGARET   There is no feeling, only the acts. Each act only multiplies
               the need. Even before the immediate act is done, even be-
               fore he reluctantly releases himself into that place I give
               to him, he is already building towards the next act.

WALLACE   What is the sensation?

MARGARET   Say it to me.

WALLACE   *At the sight of the blackbirds*

MARGARET   More slowly.

               MARGARET walks as she listens.

WALLACE   *At the sight of the blackbirds*
               Flying in a green light,
               Even the bawds of euphony
               Would cry out sharply.

MARGARET   I know that cry.

WALLACE   In the context of the poem...

MARGARET   In the context of the act of sex without love or anything
               like love.
               His sharp cry, "God damn it god damn it god damn it arghhh."
               Days of it, weeks.

WALLACE   Please-leave-me-or-I-will-die sex.

MARGARET   I give over my body. I do. Still it is not enough.

Finally he bursts. "You are so removed when I have sex with you. You are not even in your body, not even in the room."

"You give me nothing."

MARGARET stares out at the sea.

MARGARET turns and stares into the deep past.

I think of the seal hung in that green high roller backlit by the golden light of memory, the point of turning.

"You give me nothing." This is what I thought.

How do I get to be that seal? I am numb from the ache to be inside the beauty of a poem.

WALLACE   If you had written it down, made a poem that day...

MARGARET   ...Yes?

There it was. *(acknowledging)* I gave him nothing.

MARGARET holds out her emptiness.

But I answered him, "No, I am here. I promise. I am here." Three years more I pulled us through liquid glass,

shards in our wake.

a blood flecked urge to go even a step further

MARGARET   What were his last moments like?

WALLACE   I am not omnipresent, Margaret.

MARGARET   I feel John inside the smashed car smashed and the first person on the scene a young man repeatedly running up to look inside but sprinting away frightened by John's... dying moans.

WALLACE   Employ the five senses.

MARGARET   Metallic odour of the monstrous wreck, bile of a lacerated liver, his spine interrupted his fingers' tips dead, *(testing)* his spine interrupted his fingers' tips stilled—

WALLACE   —yes.

MARGARET   —slapping of sneakers on wet pavement, a young man's face a puzzle in cracked glass appearing, disappearing, re-appearing, disappearing.

John is at once the changed man trapped inside the twisted metal and the young man trying to have the courage to look inside and see the horror of that change.

The John I fell in love with loved metaphors.

> *MARGARET is walking a figure eight, always pausing where*
> *the two ovals meet. Her discoveries should coincide with the*
> *crossover.*

Stanza eleven.

WALLACE   Your nemesis.

MARGARET   Yes, I never got through it.

WALLACE   *He rode over Connecticut*
                In a glass coach.
                Once, a fear pierced him,
                In that he mistook
                The shadow of his equipage
                For blackbirds.

MARGARET   There is a trick to reading Wallace Stevens. Substitute "I,"
                whenever Stevens says "he" or "she."

WALLACE   *I rode over Connecticut*
                In a glass coach.
                Once, a fear pierced me,
                In that I mistook
                The shadow of my equipage
                For blackbirds.

> *MARGARET walks the figure eight for a long time.*

MARGARET   I am in Connecticut in a glass coach.

The faculty meet-and-greet for new Ph.D. students. I stand at the edge of the room watching. The sensations in me of beautiful poems! A brilliant thesis! Publications in scholarly journals! Tenure! I am shining with every future.

I see him, of course, in the centre of the room, the golden boy.

I think it will make a good poem... sex with this slightly drunken golden boy.

Mmmmm I like it, waking up with this glowing boy in my bed.

I tell him, "You are in bed with a woman who will one day be a famous poet for using the word scrotum beautifully in a sonnet."

She stops walking.

He rolls his body away from mine. He laughs, "A poet?"

fear pierces me

I laugh back, "After we have tenure."

We is a bold word. He takes it. "When we are Dean of Graduate Studies," he says.

In that moment, I mistook,

John laying his body along the whole of the length of me

for blackbirds.

There is the sound of blackbirds in flight. MARGARET slowly turns in place, counting them.

One, two, three, four, five, six, seven, eight, nine, ten and see, there, the eleventh lifting off.

I love this poem.

This poem holds the meaning of me. I will get to the end.

WALLACE moves towards the stairs. She stops him.

You almost killed it in me.

No.

You kept it alive in me.

Oh the pain of that.

She pauses then kisses him on the mouth tenderly, forgivingly.

I chose well.

I will get to the end of everything.

MARGARET steps back as the light on WALLACE leaks away until he is a shadow.

stanza xii
flying

WALLACE is in the shadows.

MARGARET is in a beautiful Mediterranean blue dressing gown.

MARGARET A month walking in an olive grove in Crete changes me. I bury the yellowed copy of the last email from him, "I fell out of love with you," in the sandy soil under an olive tree.

At the airport in Athens, waiting to board the plane as a passenger is a pilot. His jacket lapel has tiny metal wings to show he is a pilot. He is fifty-five, maybe, and his face looks as weary of pain as I feel. He isn't doing anything to hide it—he is simply stillness, sadness but above all he is weary. He is as aware of me as I am of him. We stand ten paces apart looking at the other when it is safe to do so. We are weary warriors from the same tribe; we don't know the face but we know the soul.

I don't know what he thinks when he looks at me but I want to touch him. Touch his wrists, hold his head, smooth the lines around his eyes and mouth with my thumbs.

MARGARET removes the bedspread from the bed.

The plane is ten then thirty minutes delayed. The current between us is steady. Anything is possible but then the stewardess—out of courtesy—comes to get him and escorts him on board first. When I enter the plane I see that he is seated at the back. We never speak. When we land he is gone. I collect my luggage. I never see him again.

MARGARET throws a beautiful red fabric over the bed.

When I am at home in bed I think of the pilot. I think of his face, his shoulders, his wrists. I remember when I looked away how it felt to feel his eyes on me. I imagine not that we sit together on the plane but that somehow by some magic we are both at the taxi stand waiting silently side by side. Still without speaking we get into the same cab. He asks if I would like to go to dinner with him but I say, "I... am... so... tired."

MARGARET sits on the side of the bed. She slides the dressing gown off her shoulders, revealing her naked back. She slides modestly between the sheets.

Then like that we are in the hotel room, naked under the sheets. I forgive myself for however it is that I came to be naked with this man with those eyes that fuel me.

MARGARET moves in the bed, curling her body.

We fold together our soft bodies radiating warmth. He takes my breasts in his hands, his lips, his breath warm on the back of my neck.

MARGARET moves her hair to expose her neck to his mouth.

I say,
"Tell me about her."

I imagine that she died of breast cancer just when they were sure she was going to live. He describes her vitality, her dark hair and how he slept with it under his head always. Tears slide out of my eyes and down my nose.

MARGARET moves as she speaks.

I move slightly so my hand can slide between our bodies. I reach down and touch his penis, which is hard with his desire for me to be her.

MARGARET does these actions as she talks. MARGARET sits on the bed in such a way that only her back is revealed in the low light.

I turn towards him and press him onto his back. I climb onto him, my hips settling on his hips. I stay upright, adjusting the pillows at his back until he can easily take my breast into his mouth.

MARGARET offers her breasts to him, first one and then the other.

And he does, his mouth so new, the feelings so buried. I begin the story of John. I describe his way of laughing and the first time I knew that I loved him. I describe the night we woke on the same breath when, at the very moment I curled my hand around his, John's light, John's dark left our bed. So long, John. *(meaning time)*

MARGARET turns her head so that her face is briefly revealed.

So long, John. *(meaning goodbye)*

She turns back.

I feel the space, my body light with it.

MARGARET's hands slide down her body and she shifts her hips a little.

His hands leave my breasts and he slides them down to my hips, lifting me until we are connected and we have poetry of sex, sex of poetry until our edges and the edges of the dark sky break with brilliant orange.

MARGARET makes a deeply pure sound as the ice cracks open.

WALLACE   *The river is moving*
               The blackbird must be flying.

stanza xiii
it was evening all afternoon

MARGARET   I hire a tradesman to bring light into my house.

And he does.

So… much… light.

I have tea ready for his breaks so that I can look at his hands cupped around the mug. He holds them out to me—turning them over and back so I can see the nicks the scars the dents of hands used to make a living.

"I am not very good with the ladies, would you like to come for a walk with me?"

We walk. He is a man who has lived his whole life pushing his body to stay upright. In the last year of his marriage he woke every morning with his arms spread eagle and numb. I tell him that it is a beautiful metaphor of a man in a loveless marriage waking each morning, his arms open to wrap around someone but empty, numb with longing.

No. I don't say it. I write it down. Not a poem. A story that wants to be a poem.

He kisses me. He says, "That was good, woman."

Woman.

He calls me "missus"—testing, I can see, how I take this
word his father said to his mother, in the way that his foot
playfully bounces newly rigged scaffolding before he gives
it his full weight to bear.

   MARGARET lies down fully clothed on the bed.

"I like your bosom," he says.

Bosom.

I feel it, a small thrill of vibration around words again.

How long has it been since I felt this?

The nerve endings on the surface of every part of my body
rise and ripple under his touch, my thoughts are iron fil-
ings rising too, to this magnet that cannot be resisted. I
let my mind go.

We walk. We capture fireflies along the shore.

We come back to my house and open the mason jars in
my bedroom. We lie on the bed watching the glimmers
of light come and go.

   Fireflies fly about the room, some land on the bedspread.

"We are inside a poem," I tell him.

"I don't know what that means," he says.

It's not a meaning, it is a sensation.

> MARGARET *gets out of the bed looking down—describes the*
> *scene so tenderly.*

My mind steps out, stands away, looking down on the bed.
I watch my body, how I move with him, how free my body
is with his. The sounds I make as his hands, oh, move along
my belly, breasts, face, hair, are joyful there is some slick-
coated animal in my chest calling out. I want words. I listen
but there is only the slow release of air from deep inside
him.

I want words.

Then...... they... come.

Thrumming.

WORDS—they brim the world, beautiful words.

I shimmer with their sounds he does not hear.

I watch my body pull free,

> MARGARET *holds out her hands, taking the hands of* MARGARET,
> *pulling her free of the bed.*

behind me his arms unfurl tendrils of his longing.

> MARGARET *leans down as though she might be pulled into the*
> *bed but she turns away. She walks to the stairs and climbs*
> *up to the desk.*

WALLACE   *It was evening all afternoon.*
               It was snowing
               And it was going to snow.
               The blackbird sat
               In the cedar-limbs.

                    MARGARET's pen drops to the page and the moment she begins
                    to write she speaks.

MARGARET   in the darkness
               the fireflies appear disappear
               appear
               the beating hearts of the words I write
               made visible.

               I love this moment. It is all I do love.

                    MARGARET writes as everything darkens, the fireflies moving
                    about.

                    WALLACE stands far out on the point like a beacon. Fireflies
                    move around him.

                    The theatre is awash with fireflies.

                    The end.

The playwright, with deep appreciation, acknowledges

The Saskatchewan Playwrights Centre Spring Festival of New Plays—director Tom Bentley-Fisher, actors Sharon Bakker and Rob Roy, dramaturges Heather Inglis and Colleen Murphy.

Tant per Tant—Elisabet Ràfols, literary director, and Tom Bentley-Fisher, artistic director.

Factory Theatre—actors Elizabeth Saunders, Rosemary Dunsmore and R.H. Thomson, dramaturge Iris Turcott and artistic director Ken Gass.

Cover artist—Karen Klee-Atlin.

Elizabeth Smart—for the title of stanza xi, which was inspired by a line in her novel *The Assumption of the Rogues and Rascals*.

Playwrights Atlantic Resource Centre—Jenny Munday.

Urban Curvz—for the workshop and their beautiful premiere of this script.

Playwrights Canada Press—Blake Sproule for his attention, care and good humour during our editing process.

Playwrights' Workshop Montréal—Lois Brown, post-production dramaturge.

Tessa Mendel (always my first reader), Pamela Halstead, Margot Dionne, John Dunsworth, Mary Vingoe, Colleen Murphy, Florence Gibson MacDonald, Ruth Lawrence, Janis Spence, Marina Endicott, Philip Adams, Paris, Leah Hamilton and Claudia Mitchell.

Love to my children.

Author photo by Michelle Doucette Design and Photography

Catherine Banks lives and writes in Nova Scotia. Some of her notable plays include *Bitter Rose*, which aired on Bravo! Canada, and *Bone Cage*, which won the Governor General's Literary Award for Drama. Catherine received Nova Scotia's Established Artist Award in 2008.